Portuguese Phrase Book

Get Fluent & Increase Your Portuguese Vocabulary, Portuguese Phrase Book for Tourist

Anna Fichter

Table of Content

Language Survival Tips

Memory Aid Techniques

Introduction

Brief Overview of Portuguese

Portuguese, one of the Sentiment languages, is spoken by a huge number of individuals overall and is the authority language of Portugal, Brazil, Mozambique, Angola, Cape Verde, Guinea-Bissau, and São Tomé and Príncipe. It is likewise a perceived local language in East Timor and Macau. This segment gives a compact prologue to the critical parts of the Portuguese language for the people who are different to it.

Historical Context

Portuguese has a rich historical foundation that follows back to the middle-age Galician-Portuguese spoken in the northwest region of the Iberian Promontory. The language developed during the Time of Disclosure when Portuguese voyagers like Vasco da Gama and Ferdinand Magellan assumed essential parts in oceanic investigation.

Language Attributes

Letter set: Portuguese proposes the Latin letter set with a couple of additional characters, for example, ç, á, é, í, ó, and ú.

Phonetics: Portuguese is a phonetic language, significant words are by and large articulated as they are composed. Notwithstanding, the pronunciation might fluctuate across various Portuguese-talking areas.

Language: Portuguese punctuation incorporates highlights like gendered things (manly and ladylike), action word formations, and subject-action word object sentence structure.

Varieties

There are two essential varieties of Portuguese:

European Portuguese: Verbally expressed in Portugal and impacted by the country's one-of-a-kind history and culture.

Brazilian Portuguese: Verbally expressed in Brazil, this variety has been affected by native languages and has unmistakable pronunciation and jargon contrasted with European Portuguese.

Pronunciation Tips
Portuguese pronunciation can be trying for fledglings, however rehearsing a few fundamental standards can essentially further develop correspondence. Central issues include:

Vowels: Portuguese has nasalized vowels, and that implies the sound is delivered through the nose.

Consonants: Focus on the pronunciation of 'r' and 'lh,' as they can be not quite the same as other Sentiment languages.

Pronunciation Guide

Dominating Portuguese pronunciation is a key stage in becoming certain and compelling in your correspondence. While it might appear to be trying from the outset, we will assist you with exploring the complexities of Portuguese sounds and further develop your communication in language abilities.

Vowels

A (ah): Like the 'a' in "father."

E (eh): Like the 'e' in "bed."

I (ee): Like the 'ee' in "see."

O (gracious): Like the 'o' in "go."

U (oo): Like the 'oo' in "food."

Nasalized Vowels:

Ã (ão): Like the 'a' in "need."
Õ (õo): Like the 'o' in "conceived."
Consonants
C:

Before 'a', 'o', or 'u', it is articulated like 'k' (e.g., "casa").
Before 'e' or 'I', it is articulated like 's' (e.g., "Cidade").
CH (ch): Articulated like the 'sh' in "she."

L:

Toward the start of a word or syllable, it is articulated like the English 'I.'
In the centre or end of a word, it tends to be velarized, like the 'll' in "million."
NH (nh): Like the 'ny' in "gorge."

R:

Toward the start of a word or after 'l', 's', or 'z', it is articulated like the 'h' in "cap."
Somewhere else, it is much of the time articulated as a throaty 'r' sound, like the French 'r'.
S:

Toward the start of a word, before a consonant, or between vowels, it is articulated like the 's' in "sun."
Toward the finish of a syllable, it tends to be articulated like the 'z' in "nothing."
SS (ss): Articulated like the 'ss' in "kiss."

X:

Toward the start of a word, it is articulated like 'z' (e.g., "xícara").
Between vowels, it is articulated like 's' (e.g., "exame").
Highlight

Focus on highlighted vowels, as they frequently demonstrate pressure and can change the pronunciation of a word.

Á, É, Í, Ó, Ú: These vowels are focused on and articulated more unmistakably than others.

Essential
Phrases

Greetings and Introductions

Graciousness and basic manners play a huge part in Portuguese culture, and dominating good tidings and presentations is fundamental for making positive communications. Whether you're meeting somebody interestingly or participating in regular discussions, the accompanying expressions will assist you with exploring the social scene in Portuguese-talking conditions.

Fundamental Good tidings

Hi:
Olá (goodness lah)

Greetings (casual):
Oi (oy)

Good day:
Bom dia (bohm dee-ah)

Good evening:
Boa tarde (boh-ah tahr-dee)

Goodbye/night:
Boa noite (boh-ah noy-ti)

Presenting Yourself

My name is...:
Meu nome é... (may-oo noh-mee eh)

I'm from...:
Eu sou de... (eh-oo soh day)

Satisfied to meet you:
Prazer em conhecê-lo/a (prah-zeir point koh-neh-say-loh/ah)

Answering Presentations

Good to meet you as well:

Prazer em conhecê-lo/a também (prah-zeir point koh-neh-say-loh/ah-tahm-behm)

Relaxed Good tidings

How are you?:
Como vai? (koh-moh vai)

I'm fine, bless your heart:
Estou bem, obrigado/a (ehs-toh bayn, goodness bree-gah-doo/dah)

What's more, you?:
E você? (ee voh-say)

Considerate Articulations

Excuse me:
Com licença (kohm lee-sen-sah)

If it's not too much trouble:
Por favor (por fah-vohr)

Goodbyes

Farewell:
Adeus (ah-deh-oos)

See you later:
Até logo (ah-teh loh-goo)

Fare thee well:
Cuide-se (kwee-deh seh)

Cultural Tip

While greeting somebody, it's not unexpected to trade a handshake or a kiss on the two cheeks, contingent upon the degree of commonality and the locale. Focus on meaningful gestures and follow the lead of the individual you are connecting with.

Common Expressions

Notwithstanding fundamental good tidings, dominating typical statements is significant for viable correspondence in Portuguese. These articulations are much of the time utilized in ordinary discussions and can assist you with exploring different social circumstances. Here are a few critical expressions to add profundity to your Portuguese language abilities:

Offering Thanks

Many thanks to you:
Obrigado (oh-bree-gah-doo) - Used by males
Obrigada (oh-bree-gah-dah) - Used by females

The pleasure is all mine:
De nothing (day nah-dah)

If it's not too much trouble:

Por favor (por fah-vohr)

Amiable Solicitations

Might you at any point help me, please?:
Você pode me ajudar, por favor? (voh-say poh-deh may ah-zoo-dar, por fah-vohr)

Excuse me, where is...?:
Com licença, onde fica...? (kohm lee-sen-sah, on-dee expense kah)

Communicating Arrangement and Conflict

Indeed:
Sim (appear)

No:
Não (presently)

I concur:
Eu concordo (eh-oo kohn-kor-doo)

I disagree:
Eu não concordo (eh-oo now kohn-kor-doo)

Requesting Explanation

Might you at some point rehash that, please?:
Você pode repetir, por favor? (voh-say poh-deh reh-peh-teer, por fah-vohr)

I don't have the foggiest idea:
Eu não entendo (eh-oo now en-ten-doo)

Communicating Shock or Fervor

Amazing!:
Uau! (wau)

Phenomenal!:
Fantástico/a! (fahn-tahs-tee-koo/kah)

Regular Civilities

Good day, evening, evening:
Bom dia, boa tarde, boa noite (bohm dee-ah, boh-ah tahr-dee, boh-ah noy-ti)

Please accept my apologies:
Desculpe (deh-skool-peh)

Favour you (after sniffling):
Saúde (sow-deh)

Mingling

What's your name?:
Como você se chama? (koh-moh voh-say seh shah-mah)

Ideal to meet you:
Prazer em conhecê-lo/a (prah-zeir point koh-neh-say-loh/ah)

These typical statements will work well for you in different circumstances, from offering thanks to exploring everyday communications.

Polite Requests and Responses

Courteousness is a vital part of Portuguese correspondence, and utilizing pleasant solicitations and reactions is fundamental for laying out sure connections. Whether you're looking for help or making a solicitation, utilizing polite language improves the nature of your correspondence. Here are a few considerate expressions for making demands and comparing reactions:

Making Amiable Solicitations:

Might you at some point kindly assist me?:
Você poderia me ajudar, por favor? (voh-say poh-deh-ree-ah meh ah-zoo-dar, por fah-vohr)

Could it be conceivable to...?:
Seria possível...? (seh-ree-ah poh-see-vehl)

May I pose you an inquiry?:
Posso fazer-lhe uma pergunta? (poh-so fah-zer-lhe oo-mah per-thug tah)

Could you sympathetic explain...?:
Você poderia explicar gentilmente...? (voh-say poh-dee-ree-ah ehks-plee-vehicle jen-teel-men-te)

I would see the value in it if...:
Eu agradeceria se... (eh-oo ah-grah-deh-seh-ree-ah seh)

Amiable Reactions:

I'd be eager to assist:
Certamente, ficarei feliz em ajudar (sehr-teh-men-te, charge cah-beam expense leez point ah-zoo-dar)

Go ahead and inquire:

Claro, sinta-se à vontade para perguntar (kla-roh, seen-tah-seh ah vohn-tah-deh pah-ra per-thug tar)

I'll put forth a valiant effort to help you: Farei o meu melhor para ajudar você (fah-rei gracious meh-oo meh-lhor pah-ra ah-zoo-dar voh-say)

Here's the data you really want: Certamente, aqui está an informação que você precisa (sehr-teh-men-te, ah-kee es-tah ah in-for-mah-sow khe voh-say preh-ee-sah)

I'd be glad to make sense of: Ficarei feliz em explicar (charge cah-beam expense leez point ehks-plee-vehicle)

Extra Respectfulness Tips:

Use "Por Favor" Generously: The expression "por favor" (if it's not too much trouble, can be added to practically any solicitation to convey pleasantness. For instance, "Posso ter um bistro, por favor?" (Could I at any point have an espresso, please?).

Express Appreciation: When somebody helps you, it is standard to offer thanks. Saying "Obrigado/a" (thank you) in the wake of getting help is a courteous and valued signal.

Be Deferential of Time: While making demands, recognize the other individual's time by utilizing phrases like "Quando for conveniente para você?" (When is helpful for you?) to show thought.

By integrating these pleasant expressions into your discussions, you'll impart as well as add to a positive and conscious environment. Neighborliness is a widespread language that rises above cultural limits, and it's an important resource in any friendly or expert setting.

Thanking and Apologizing

Here are typical statements for expressing gratitude toward and saying 'sorry' alongside cultural insights:

Expressing gratitude toward in Portuguese:

Many thanks to you:
Obrigado (oh-bree-gah-doo) - Used by males
Obrigada (oh-bree-gah-dah) - Used by females

You're the best:
Muito obrigado/a (moo-ee-toh gracious bree-gah-doo/dah) - "Muito" signifies "a great deal" or "very."

Thank you kindly:
Muito obrigado/a mesmo (moo-ee-toh gracious bree-gah-doo/dah meh-smoo)

I feel a debt of gratitude:

Eu agradeço (eh-oo ah-grah-deh-soo)

Gratitude for your assistance:
Obrigado/a pela sua ajuda (gracious bree-gah-doo/dah peh-lah soo ah-zoo-dah)

Saying 'sorry' in Portuguese:

Please accept my apologies:
Desculpe (deh-skool-peh) - Regularly utilized for casual conciliatory sentiments
Desculpa (deh-skool-pah) - Likewise utilized casually

I am sorry:
Eu peço desculpas (eh-oo peh-soo deh-skool-pahs)

Please accept my apologies for...:
Sinto muito por... (seen-toh moo-ee-toh poor)

Kindly excuse me:

Por favor, me perdoe (por fah-vohr, meh pehr-doh-eh)

I didn't mean to...:
Eu não quis dizer... (eh-oo now kees dee-zer)

Cultural Insights:
Appreciation and Correspondence: Communicating thanks is a fundamental social show in Portuguese-talking societies. It reflects an appreciation for the endeavours or thoughtfulness shown. Answering with "de nothing" (the pleasure is all mine) is a typical method for responding the appreciation.

Saying 'sorry' with Earnestness: While saying 'sorry' truthfulness is critical. Adding "mesmo" (truly) as in "Desculpe mesmo" or "Sinto muito mesmo" stresses authentic lament. Recognizing your mix-up and showing a genuine craving to set things right is culturally esteemed.

Getting Around

Asking for Directions

Exploring new spots turns out to be a lot smoother when you can unhesitatingly request headings. In Portuguese-talking districts, looking for direction is a typical and invited communication.

Essential Expressions:

Excuse me, where is...?:
Com licença, onde fica...? (kohm lee-sen-sah, on-dee expense kah)

Could you at any point let me know how to get to...?:
Você pode me dizer como chegar a...? (voh-say poh-deh meh day-zer koh-moh shay-gar ah...)

Is it not even close to here?:
É longe daqui? (eh lohn-hmm dah-kee)

What direction to...?:
Qual é o caminho para...? (kwahl eh oo kah-mee-nyoo pah-rah)

Milestones and Spots:

The exhibition hall:
O museu (oo moo-zay-oo)

The train station:
An estação de trem (ah es-tah-sawn jee trehng)

The bus station:
O ponto de ônibus (oo pohn-toh jee gracious nee-transport)

The downtown area:
O centro da cidade (oo sen-troh dah see-dah-dee)

Getting Explanations:

Might you at any point show me on the guide?:
Você pode me mostrar no mapa? (voh-say poh-deh meh mohs-trahr noh mah-pah)

Is it to the left or right?:
É à esquerda ou à direita? (eh ah es-kehr-dah oo ah dee-rey-tah)

Helpful Expressions for Explanation:

Straight ahead:
Em frente (eng frehn-teh)

Turn left:
Vire à esquerda (vee-rey ah es-kehr-dah)

Turn right:
Vire à direita (vee-rey ah dee-rey-tah)

Go past the...:
Old fashioned por... (pah-seh poor)

Transportation Vocabulary

Exploring transportation in a Portuguese-talking locale turns out to be more reasonable when you know all about the fundamental jargon connected with travel. Whether you're utilizing public transportation or looking for bearings, these expressions will demonstrate helpful:

Well-known Methods of Transportation:

Vehicle:
Carro (kah-hoo)

Transport:
Ônibus (gracious nee-boos)

Train:
Trem (trehng)

Tram/Metro:
Metrô (meh-troh)

Taxi:
Táxi (tahk-see)

Bike:
Bicicleta (honey bee see-kleh-tah)

Strolling:
A pé (ah peh)

Transportation Offices:

Air terminal:
Aeroporto (ah-eh-roh-pohr-as well)

Train Station:
Estação de trem (es-tah-sawn jee trehng)

Transport Stop:
Ponto de ônibus (pohn-toh jee goodness nee-transport)

Port:

Porto (pohr-as well)

Headings and Travel Expressions:

Where is the train station?:
Onde fica an estação de trem? (on-dee charge kah ah es-tah-sawn jee trehng)

How much is a ticket to...?:
Quanto custa um bilhete para...? (kwahn-toh koos-tah oong honey bee yeh-teh pah-rah)

Is it nowhere near here?:
É longe daqui? (eh lohn-hmm dah-kee)

Which stage for the train to...?:
Qual plataforma para o trem com destino a...? (kwahl plah-tah-for-mah pah-rah oo trehng kohng des-tee-noh ah)

Traveling via Vehicle:

Service station:

Posto de gasolina (pohs-too jee gah-zoh-lee-nah)

Gridlock:
Engarrafamento (eng-gah-hah-fah-men-toh)

Roadway:
Rodovia (hoh-doh-vee-ah)

Helpful Expressions:

Might you at any point suggest a decent transportation administration?:
Você pode recomendar um bom serviço de transporte? (voh-say poh-deh heh-koh-men-dar oong bohng sehr-vee-soo jee trans-pohr-te)

I want a guide of the city:
Preciso de um mapa da cidade (preh-see-zoh deh oong mah-pah dah see-dah-dee)

Numbers and Counting

Learning numbers in Portuguese is fundamental for different circumstances, from shopping and eating to saying what time it is and giving bearings. Here is a complete guide to numbers including in Portuguese:

Cardinal Numbers (0-20):

Zero: Zero
One: Um
Two: Dois
Three: Três
Four: Quatro
Five: Cinco
Six: Seis
Seven: Sete
Eight: Oito
Nine: Nove
Ten: Dez
Eleven: Onze

Twelve: Rest
Thirteen: Treze
Fourteen: Catorze
Fifteen: Quinze
Sixteen: Dezesseis
Seventeen: Dezessete
Eighteen: Dezoito
Nineteen: Dezenove
Multiples of Ten:
Twenty: Vinte
Thirty: Trinta
Forty: Quarenta
Fifty: Cinquenta
Sixty: Sessenta
Seventy: Setenta
Eighty: Oitenta
Ninety: Noventa

Hundreds:

100: Cem
200: Duzentos/as
300: Trezentos/as

400: Quatrocentos/as
500: Quinhentos/as
600: Seiscentos/as
700: Setecentos/as
800: Oitocentos/as
900: Novecentos/as

Thousands and more:

1,000. 1,000: Mil
2,000. 2,000: Dois Mil
10,000. 10,000: Dez Mil
100,000. 100,000: Cem Mil
a million. 1,000,000: Um Milhão

Ordinal Numbers:

First: Primeiro/a
Second: Segundo/a
Third: Terceiro/a
Fourth: Quarto/a
Fifth: Quinto/a
6th: Sexto/a

Seventh: Sétimo/a
Eighth: Oitavo/a
10th: Nono/a
10th: Décimo/a

Counting Tips:

While counting objects, utilize the manly structure for numbers finishing off with "o" (e.g., dois livros - two books) and the ladylike structure for numbers finishing in "a" (e.g., duas plateaus - two tables).

In bigger numbers, the combination "e" is utilized to associate units and tens (e.g., vinte e cinco - 25).

At costs and amounts, utilize "reais" for Brazilian cash (e.g., dez reais - ten Brazilian reais) and "euros" for European money.

Cultural Note:

Understanding numbers is essential for everyday exercises like shopping, paying for administrations, and giving the current time. Also, monitoring cultural subtleties in mathematical articulations can upgrade your correspondence and reconciliation inside Portuguese-talking networks. Work on counting consistently to fortify your language abilities and assemble trust in different situations.

Accommodation

Checking into a Hotel

When looking into a hotel in a Portuguese-talking district, successful openness is of the utmost importance for guaranteeing a smooth and wonderful experience. Get to know these fundamental expressions to make the registration cycle more direct:

Appearance and Hello:

Hi, I have a booking:
Olá, eu tenho uma reserva. (goodness lah, eh-oo ten-yoo oo-mah reh-zehr-vah)

My name is...:
Meu nome é... (may-oo noh-mee eh...)

I might want to register:
Eu gostaria de fazer o registration. (eh-oo gohs-tah-ree-ah deh fah-zer oo registration)

Giving Data:

Here is my ID/Visa:
Aqui está meu RG/Passaporte. (ok kee es-tah may-oo eh-je/Passa-por-ti)

I have a booking under the name...:
Eu tenho uma reserva em nome de... (eh-oo ten-yoo oo-mah reh-zehr-vah eng noh-mee deh...)

Room Inclinations:

I would like a solitary/twofold room:
Eu gostaria de um quarto de solteiro/casal. (eh-oo gohs-tah-ree-ah deh oong kwahr-toh deh sohl-tay-roo/kah-sahl)

May I have a room with a view?:
Posso ter um quarto com vista? (poh-so tay oong kwahr-toh kohm vee-stah)

Are there any suitable redesigns?:

Há alguma opção de redesign disponível? (ok ahl-goo-mah ohp-sawn deh up-dim di dis-pon-ee-vehl)

Length and Installment:

I will remain for... evenings:
Vou ficar por... noites. (voh fih-vehicle poor... noy-tis)

How much is the room each evening?:
Quanto custa o quarto por noite? (kwahn-toh koos-tah oo kwahr-toh poor noy-ti)

Is breakfast included?:
O bistro da manhã está incluído? (oo kah-fey dah mahn-yah eh-stah een-kloo-ee-doo)

Might I at any point pay with a Visa?:

Posso pagar com cartão de crédito? (poh-so pah-gar kohm kar-towm deh kreh-dee-to)

Extra Demands:

I want a reminder at...:
Eu preciso de uma chamada para acordar às... (eh-oo preh-see-zoh deh oo-mah sha-mah-da pah-rah ah-kor-dar ahs...)

Might I at any point have additional towels/toiletries?:
Eu poderia ter toalhas/produtos de higiene additional items? (eh-oo po-deh-ree-ah tehr twa-lhas/proh-doo-tos deh ee-zhee-en-ee ehks-trahs)

Shutting the Collaboration:

Many thanks to you for your help:

Obrigado/a pela sua assistência. (gracious
bree-gah-doo/dah peh-lah soo
ah-see-sten-syah)

Partake in your visit:
Tenha uma boa estadia. (ten-yah oo-mah
bo-ah es-tah-dee-ah)

Asking for Basic Services

At the point when you're in a Portuguese-talking district and need explicit administration, compelling correspondence is fundamental. Here are expressions to assist you with requesting fundamental administrations and make your solicitations understood and respectful:

In an Eatery or Bistro:

May I see the menu, please?:
Posso ver o cardápio, por favor? (poh-so vehr oo kar-dah-pyoo, por fah-vor)

Might I at some point have the bill, please?:
Posso ter a conta, por favor? (poh-so tayr ah kohn-tah, por fah-vor)

Is there a veggie lover choice?:

Tem alguma opção vegetariana? (tem ahl-goo-mah ohp-sawn veh-zhee-tah-ree-ah-nah)

In a Store:

Excuse me, where can I find...?:
Com licença, onde posso encontrar...? (kohm lee-sen-sah, on-deh poh-so en-kon-trar)

Do you have this in an alternate size/variety?:
Você tem isso em um tamanho/cor diferente? (voh-say tem ee-soh eng oong tah-mahn-yo/kor dee-feh-rehn-tee)

What amount does this cost?:
Quanto custa isso? (kwahn-toh koos-tah ee-so)

At a Hotel or Convenience:

Might I at some point get additional pads/covers?:
Posso ter travesseiros/cobertores additional items? (poh-so tayr trah-veh-say-roos/koh-ber-toh-res ehk-trahs)

Is there a reminder administration?:
Tem serviço de despertar? (tem sehr-vee-soo deh-spehr-tar)

Might I at any point have a late checkout?:
Posso fazer o checkout mais tarde? (poh-so fah-zer oo look at mah-ees tahr-de)

Transportation Administrations:

Might you at any point call a taxi for me, please?:
Você pode chamar um táxi para mim, por favor? (voh-say poh-dee sha-deface oong tahk-see pah-rah meem, por fah-vor)

Is there a transport/metro stop close by?:

Tem algum ponto de ônibus/metrô por perto? (tem ahl-goom pohntoo jee goodness nee-transport/meh-troh poor pehr-toh)

What time does the following train/transport leave?:
A que horas sai o próximo trem/ônibus? (ok keh gracious ras sah-ee oo proh-ksy-moo trehng/goodness nee-boos)

General Administrations:

Where is the closest drug store?:
Onde fica a farmácia mais próxima? (on-dee expense kah ah fahr-mah-see-ah mah-ees noh-mah)

Do you give Wi-Fi here?:
Vocês oferecem Wi-Fi aqui? (voh-says gracious fey-reh-saym Wi-Fi ah-kee)

Might I at any point have an additional key, please?:

Posso ter uma chave extra, por favor? (poh-so tayr oo-mah sha-veh ehk-trah, por fah-vor)

Crisis Administrations:

Is there a clinic close by?:
Tem algum emergency clinic por perto? (tem ahl-goom goodness spee-tahl poor pehr-toh)

I really want to call the police. Where is the closest station?:
Preciso chamar a polícia. Onde é a delegacia mais próxima? (preh-see-zoh sha-deface ah po-lee-see-ah. on-deh eh ah deh-leh-gah-see-ah mah-ees noh-mah)

Could you at any point assist me with tracking down a nearby international haven?:
Você pode me ajudar an encontrar uma embaixada neighborhood? (voh-say poh-deh

meh ah-zoo-dar ah en-kon-trar oo-mah
em-bah-ee-sah-dah loh-kahl)

Cultural Tips:
Good manners Matters: Begin your
solicitation with "Com licença" (Excuse me)
and end it with "por favor" (please) to
convey consideration.

Common Phrases for Staying Overnight

Here are well-known expressions to assist you with exploring your convenience and guarantee an agreeable stay:

Checking In:

Hi, I have a booking:

Olá, eu tenho uma reserva. (goodness lah, eh-oo ten-yoo oo-mah reh-zehr-vah)
My name is...:
Meu nome é... (may-oo noh-mee eh...)

I might want to register:
Eu gostaria de fazer o registration. (eh-oo gohs-tah-ree-ah deh fah-zer oo registration)

Room Requests:

What time is look at tomorrow?:

A que horas é o look at amanhã? (ok keh goodness ras eh oo look at ah-mahn-yah)

Is breakfast included?:
O bistro da manhã está incluído? (oo kah-fey dah mahn-yah eh-stah een-kloo-ee-doo)

Might I at any point have a reminder at...?:
Posso ter uma chamada para acordar às...? (poh-so tayr oo-mah sha-mah-da pah-rah ah-kor-dar ahs...)

Mentioning Administrations:

Could I at any point get additional towels/covers?:
Posso ter toalhas/cobertores additional items? (poh-so tayr twa-lhas/koh-ber-toh-res ehk-trahs)

Is there a rec center/pool accessible?:

Tem the scholarly community/piscina disponível? (tem ah-ka-day-mee-ah/pees-see-nah dis-pon-ee-vehl)

Might you at any point suggest a decent neighborhood café?:
Você pode recomendar um bom restaurante neighborhood? (voh-say poh-deh heh-koh-men-dar oong bohng reh-stau-ran-te loh-kahl)

If there should be an occurrence of Issues:

There's an issue with the...:
Há um problema com o/a... (ok oong proh-bleh-mah kohm oo/ah...)

The Wi-Fi isn't working:
O Wi-Fi não está funcionando. (oo Wi-Fi now eh-stah foo-see-gracious nan-doo)

The cooling/it isn't attempting to warm:

O ar-condicionado/aquecimento não está funcionando.   (oo ahr-kohn-dee-syo-nya-do/ah-keh-shee-men-t oh now eh-stah foo-see-goodness nan-doo)

Offering Thanks:

Much thanks to you for your help:
Obrigado/a pela sua assistência. (gracious bree-gah-doo/dah   peh-lah   soo ah-see-sten-syah)

I value your assistance:
Eu agradeço pela sua ajuda. (eh-oo ah-grah-deh-soo peh-lah soo ah-oo-dah)

Checking Out:

What time is check-out?:
A que horas é o check-out? (ah keh oh-ras eh oo check-out)

Might I at any point have the bill, please?:

Posso ter a conta, por favor? (poh-so tayr ah kohn-tah, por fah-vor)

Might you at any point call a taxi for me?:
Você pode chamar um táxi para mim? (voh-say poh-dee sha-deface oong tahk-see pah-rah meem)

Shutting the Interaction:

Partake in your visit:
Tenha uma boa estadia. (ten-yah oo-mah bo-ah es-tah-dee-ah)

Much obliged to you for your neighborliness:
Obrigado/a pela sua hospitalidade. (goodness bree-gah-doo/dah peh-lah soo-ah gracious spee-tah-li-da-de)

Farewell, have an extraordinary day:
Adeus, tenha um ótimo dia. (ok deh-oos, ten-yah oong Goodness tee-moh dee-ah)

Cultural Tips:

Formal Location: It's standard to address hotel staff officially utilizing "você" and titles like "senhor" (Mr.) or "senhora" (Mrs.) except if welcome to utilize more casual language.

Dining Out

Ordering Food and Drinks

Investigating the culinary pleasures of a Portuguese-talking district is a wonderful encounter. Find out more about these expressions to arrange food and beverages at cafés and bistros with certainty:

In a Café or Bistro:

Hi, a table for two, please:
Olá, uma plateau para dois, por favor. (goodness lah, oo-mah meh-sah pah-rah doysh, por fah-vor)

May I see the menu, please?:
Posso ver o cardápio, por favor? (poh-so vehr oo kar-dah-pyoo, por fah-vor)

I might want to arrange now:
Eu gostaria de fazer o pedido marketplace. (eh-oo gohs-tah-ree-ah deh fah-zer oo peh-dee-doo ah-go-rah)

Requesting Food:

I would like the...:
Eu gostaria do(a)... (eh-oo gohs-tah-ree-ah doo/dah)

Could I at any point have it without...?:
Posso ter sem...? (poh-so tayr sehng...)

Is it zesty?:
É apimentado? (eh ah-pee-men-tah-doo)

I'm a vegan:
Sou vegetariano/a. (soh veh-zhee-tah-ree-ah-noh/ah)

I'm unfavourably susceptible to...:
Eu tenho alergia a... (eh-oo ten-yoo ah-lehr-zhee-ah ah...)

Requesting Beverages:

I would like a...:
Eu gostaria de um/uma... (eh-oo gohs-tah-ree-ah deh oong/oo-mah...)

Still water/Shimmering water:
Água sem gás/Com gás (ah-gwah sehm gahs/kohng gahs)

A glass of red/white wine:
Um copo de vinho tinto/branco (oong koh-crap deh vee-nyoo high schooler toh/brahn-koo)

What do you suggest?:
O que você recomenda? (oo keh voh-say heh-koh-men-dah)

Unique Solicitations:

Could I at any point have the dressing/sauce as an afterthought?:
Posso ter o molho à parte? (poh-so tayr oo moh-lyoo ah pahr-teh)

Might you at some point make it less/more fiery?:
Você poderia fazer menos/mais apimentado? (voh-say poh-dee-ree-ah fah-zer mehng/mahys ah-pee-men-tah-doo)

Is it conceivable to modify my request?:
É possível personalizar meu pedido? (eh pee-ssih-vel per-soh-nah-lee-zar mayoo peh-dee-doo)

Taking care of the Bill:

May I have the bill, please?:
Posso ter a conta, por favor? (poh-so tayr ah kohn-tah, por fah-vor)

Could we at any point have separate checks?:
Podemos ter contas separadas? (poh-deh-mos tayr kohn-tahs seh-pah-rah-dahs)

Do you acknowledge charge cards?:
Aceitam cartões de crédito? (ok say-tahm kar-tohns deh kreh-dee-to)

Communicating Fulfillment:

It was scrumptious, much obliged:
Estava delicioso, obrigado/a. (ehs-tah-vah deh-lee-syo-soh, goodness bree-gah-doo/dah)

The help was superb:
O serviço foi excelente. (oo sehr-vee-soh foh-ee ehk-seh-len-teh)

Cultural Tips:
Tipping Society: In numerous Portuguese-talking nations, tipping is valued however may not be pretty much as standard as in a few different locales. Gathering together the bill or leaving a little tip is normal.

Special Dietary Requests

At the point when you have explicit dietary necessities or limitations, it's essential to convey them obviously while requesting food. Here are expressions to assist you with conveying unique dietary solicitations in a Portuguese-talking locale:

Normal Dietary Solicitations:

I'm a vegan:
Eu sou vegetariano/a. (eh-oo soh veh-zhee-tah-ree-ah-noh/ah)

I don't eat meat:
Eu não como carne. (eh-oo now koh-moh kahr-neh)

I'm hypersensitive to...:
Eu tenho alergia a... (eh-oo ten-yoo ah-lehr-zhee-ah ah...)

I can't have gluten:
Não posso comer glúten. (presently poh-so koh-mehr gloo-ten)

I'm lactose-prejudiced:
Eu sou intolerante à lactose. (eh-oo soh een-toh-leh-rahn-te ah lahk-toh-zeh)

I have a nut sensitivity:
Eu tenho alergia a frutos secos. (eh-oo ten-yoo ah-lehr-zhee ah froo-tos seh-kos)

Tweaking Your Request:

Could I at any point have the dressing/sauce as an afterthought?:
Posso ter o molho à parte? (poh-so tayr oo moh-lyoo ah pahr-teh)

Might you at some point make it less/more hot?:

Você poderia fazer menos/mais apimentado? (voh-say poh-dee-ree-ah fah-zer mehng/mahys ah-pee-men-tah-doo)

Is it conceivable to redo my request?:
É possível personalizar meu pedido? (eh pee-ssih-vel per-soh-nah-lee-zar mayoo peh-dee-doo)

Sensitivities and Limitations:

I have a gluten sensitivity:
Tenho alergia a glúten. (ten-yoo ah-lehr-zhee ah gloo-ten)

I can't eat dairy items:
Não posso comer produtos lácteos. (presently poh-so koh-mehr proh-doo-tos lah-kteh-ohs)

Is this dish free from...?:
Este prato é livre de...? (ehs-teh prah-toh eh lee-vreh deh...)

Looking for Proposals:

Do you have any vegetarian choices?:
Vocês têm opções veganas? (voh-says tehm ohp-sawnz vey-gah-nahs)

What dishes do you suggest for somebody with sensitivities?:
Quais pratos você recomenda para alguém com alergias? (kwah-ees prah-tos voh-say heh-koh-men-dah pah-rah ahl-pearl kohm ah-lehr-zhee-ahs)

Cultural Tips:
Utilize Clear Language: Express your dietary limitations utilizing direct language. If conceivable, learn explicit terms connected with your dietary necessities in Portuguese.

Paying the Bill

At the point when it comes time to settle the bill at an eatery or bistro in a Portuguese-talking locale, it's useful to know how to convey instalments. Here are expressions to help you in taking care of the bill without a hitch:

Mentioning the Bill:

May I have the bill, please?:
Posso ter a conta, por favor? (poh-so tayr ah kohn-tah, por fah-vor)

Might you at some point present to us the check?:
Você poderia trazer a conta para nós? (voh-say poh-dee-ree-ah plate zehr ah kohn-tah pah-rah noys)

We're prepared to pay now:

Estamos prontos para pagar marketplace. (es-tah-mos prohn-tos pah-rah pah-gar ah-go-rah)

Requesting Separate Bills:

Might we at any point have separate checks?:
Podemos ter contas separadas? (poh-deh-mos tayr kohn-tahs seh-pah-rah-dahs)

Separate bills, please:
Contas separadas, por favor. (kohn-tahs seh-pah-rah-dahs, por fah-vor)

Asking About Installment Choices:

Do you acknowledge charge cards?:
Aceitam cartões de crédito? (ok say-tahm kar-tohns deh kreh-dee-to)

Is it conceivable to pay with cash?:

É possível pagar em dinheiro? (eh pee-ssih-vel pah-gar eng dee-ney-roo)

Do you take [currency]?:
Aceitam [currency]? (ok say-tahm [currency])

Offering Thanks:

Much thanks to you for the magnificent assistance:
Obrigado/a pelo excelente serviço. (goodness bree-gah-doo/dah peh-loh ehk-seh-len-teh sehr-vee-soo)

Much obliged to you, we partook in the feast:
Obrigado/a, nós gostamos da refeição. (goodness bree-gah-doo/dah, noys gohs-tah-mos dah heh-fey-shee-own)

Adding a Tip:

Hold onto whatever's left:
Pode ficar com o troco. (poh-deh expense kahr kohm oo troh-koo)

I might want to leave a tip:
Eu gostaria de deixar uma gorjeta. (eh-oo gohs-tah-ree-ah deh-ee-shar oo-mah gor-zheh-tah)

Arranging the Bill:

Is there a help charge included?:
Já está incluída a taxa de serviço? (zhah eh-stah een-kloo-ee-da ah tah-shah deh sehr-vee-soo)

Might you at some point kindly twofold really look at the bill?:
Você poderia conferir a conta, por favor? (voh-say poh-dee-ree-ah kohn-feh-reer ah kohn-tah, por fah-vor)

Shutting the Interaction:

Much obliged to you for the great experience:
Obrigado/a pela experiência maravilhosa. (goodness bree-gah-doo/dah peh-lah ehk-speh-ree-ehn-syah mah-rah-vee-loh-zah)

Farewell and have an extraordinary day:
Adeus, tenha um ótimo dia. (ok deh-oos, ten-yah oong Goodness tee-moh dee-ah)

Shopping

Basic Shopping Phrases

Whether you're investigating neighbourhood markets or shopping in a shopping centre, realizing some essential shopping phrases in Portuguese will upgrade your experience. Here are fundamental expressions to assist you with exploring shopping circumstances:

Entering a Store:

Hi, how are you?:
Olá, como você está? (goodness lah, koh-moo voh-say es-tah)

Excuse me, where can I find...?:
Com licença, onde posso encontrar...? (kohm lee-sen-sah, on-deh poh-so en-kon-trar)

Do you have this in an alternate size/variety?:

Você tem isso em um tamanho/cor diferente? (voh-say tehm ee-soh eng oong tah-mahn-yo/kor dee-feh-rehn-tee)

Asking About Items:

What amount does this cost?:
Quanto custa isso? (kwahn-toh koos-tah ee-so)

Is there a rebate?:
Tem algum desconto? (tem ahl-goom dehs-kon-to)

What is the merchandise exchange?:
Qual é a política de devolução? (kwahl eh ah po-leh-see-ah deh-voh-loo-sao)

Communicating Interest:

I'm simply perusing, much obliged:

Estou só dando uma olhada, obrigado/a. (es-toh soh dahndoo oo-mah gracious lah-dah, goodness bree-gah-doo/dah)

I truly like this, it's lovely:
Eu realmente gosto disso, é lindo/a. (eh-oo re-ahl-men-teh gohs-too dees-along these lines, eh leen-doo/dah)

Making a Buy:

I might want to purchase this:
Eu gostaria de comprar isso. (eh-oo gohs-tah-ree-ah deh kohm-prar ee-so)

Could I at any point pay with a Mastercard?:
Posso pagar com cartão de crédito? (poh-so pah-gar kohm kar-towm deh kreh-dee-to)

Do you acknowledge cash?:
Aceitam dinheiro? (ok say-tahm dee-ney-ro)

Arranging and Explaining:

Is there a guarantee for this item?:
Tem garantia para este produto? (tem gah-rahn-tee-ah pah-rah es-teh proh-doo-to)

Could you at any point give me a superior cost?:
Você pode me dar um preço melhor? (voh-say poh-deh meh dar oong preh-so meh-lor)

Shutting the Exchange:

Much thanks to you for your assistance:
Obrigado/a pela sua ajuda. (gracious bree-gah-doo/dah peh-lah soo ah-oo-dah)

I'll take it:
Vou levar. (voh leh-var)

Requesting a Sack or Receipt:

Might I at any point have a pack, please?:
Posso ter um saco, por favor? (poh-so tayr
oong sah-koo, por fah-vor)

May I have a receipt?:
Posso ter um recibo? (poh-so tayr oong
reh-see-boo)

Bargaining and Prices

Haggling can be a cultural standard in numerous Portuguese-talking locales. Here are expressions to assist you with arranging costs and exploring the specialty of haggling:

Starting Dealing:

Is there space for discussion?:
Tem espaço para negociação? (tem eh-pah-soo pah-rah ne-go-syah-sawn)

Might you at any point offer a superior cost?:
Você pode oferecer um preço melhor? (voh-say poh-deh gracious feh-reh-ser oong preh-so meh-lor)

Is there a markdown for cash?:

Tem desconto para pagamento em dinheiro? (tem dehs-kon-to pah-rah pah-gah-men-toh eng dee-ney-ro)

Asking About the Cost:

What amount does this cost?:
Quanto custa isso? (kwahn-toh koos-tah ee-so)

Is this the best value you can offer?:
Esse é o melhor preço que você pode oferecer? (eh-seh eh o meh-lor preh-so keh voh-say poh-deh goodness feh-reh-ser)

Communicating Interest however, Wavering:

I truly like it, yet at the same it's a piece costly:
Eu realmente gosto, mas é um pouco caro. (eh-oo re-ahl-men-teh gohs-toh, mahs eh oong po-koo kah-ro)

I don't know, let me consider it:
Não tenho certeza, deixe-me pensar.
(presently tehn-yoo sehr-tey-za, deh-ee-te
meh pen-sar)

Arranging the Cost:

Might you at some point bring down the
value a bit?:
Você poderia baixar o preço um pouco?
(voh-say poh-dee-ree-ah bye-xar o preh-so
oong po-koo)

What's the least value you can do?:
Qual é o preço mais baixo que você pode
fazer? (kwahl eh o preh-so mahys bye-xoo
keh voh-say poh-dee fah-zer)

Making a Counteroffer:

What about... [suggest your price]?:

Que tal... [sugira seu preço]? (keh tahl... [soo-zhee-rah seu preh-so])

I can offer... [state your counteroffer]?:
Posso oferecer... [diga sua contraoferta]? (poh-so goodness feh-reh-ser... [dee-gah soo-ah kohn-trah-goodness fehr-tah])

Settling the Arrangement:

Assuming that you incorporate [additional item], I'll take it:
Se incluir [item adicional], eu aceito. (seh een-kloo-eer [ee-tem ah-dee-syo-nyal], eh-oo ah-say-to)

Okay, I'll take it for [agreeable price]:
Está bem, eu aceito por [preço acordado]. (ehs-tah behn, eh-oo ah-share with poor [preh-so ah-kor-dah-doo])

Sizes and Colors

While looking for apparel or portraying things, knowing the words and expressions for sizes and tones is fundamental. Here is a guide to assist you with imparting successfully in Portuguese:

Sizes (Tamanhos):

Small:
Pequeno (Peh-kay-no)

Medium:
Médio (Meh-dee-oo)

Large:
Grande (Grahn-dee)

Extra Large:
Extra Grande (Eks-trah Grahn-dee)

Size:

Tamanho (Tah-mahn-yo)

What size do you have?:
Que tamanho você tem? (Keh tah-mahn-yo voh-say tem)

Colours (Centers):

Variety:
Cor (Kor)

Dark:
Preto (Preh-to)

White:
Branco (Brahn-koo)

Dark:
Cinza (Seen-zah)

Red:
Vermelho (Ver-meh-lyoo)

Blue:
Azul (Ah-zool)

Green:
Verde (Vehr-dee)

Yellow:
Amarelo (Ah-mah-reh-lo)

Orange:
Laranja (La-rahn-zhah)

Pink:
Rosa (Ho-sah)

Purple:
Roxo (Ho-shoo)

Brown:
Marrom (Mah-rohm)

Taking a stab at Garments:

Could I at any point give this a shot?:
Posso experimentar isso? (Poh-so
ehk-speh-ree-men-tar ee-so)

The fitting room:
O provador (O proh-vah-dor)

It fits well:
Serve bem (Ser-veh beyn)

It's excessively close/free:
Está muito apertado/folgado (Ehs-tah
mwee-toh ah-pehr-tah-doo/fohl-gah-doo)

Requesting Help:

Do you have this in another variety?:
Você tem isso em outra cor? (Voh-say tem
ee-so eng goodness tra kor)

Could you at any point assist me with
tracking down my size?:

Você pode me ajudar an encontrar meu tamanho? (Voh-say poh-deh meh ah-zoo-dar ah en-kon-trar mayoo tah-mahn-yo)

What sizes are accessible?:
Quais tamanhos estão disponíveis? (Kwah-ees tah-mahn-yos es-tah-o dee-spon-ee-vehys)

Communicating Inclinations:

I favor more obscure/lighter tones:
Prefiro centers mais escuras/mais claras (Preh-expense ro kor-ees mahys ehs-koo-rahs/myss klah-rahs)

I like dynamic tones:
Gosto de centers vibrantes (Gohs-toh deh kor-ees vee-wheat tes)

I'm searching for something in pastel tones:

Estou procurando algo em centers pastel
(Ehs-toh favorable to koo-ran-do ahl-goo eng
kor-ees pahs-tehl)

Emergency Situations

Medical Emergencies

In the lamentable case of a health-related crisis while in a Portuguese-talking district, it's critical to have the option to impart your requirements and look for help immediately. Here are expressions to help you in such circumstances:

Looking for Critical Help:

Help! I want a specialist:
Socorro! Preciso de um médico! (So-koh-roh! Preh-see-soh deh oong meh-dee-koo)

Call a rescue vehicle, please:
Chame uma ambulância, por favor. (Sha-meh oo-mah ahm-boo-lahn-syah, por fah-vor)

I've had a mishap:

Eu tive um acidente. (Eh-oo tee-vey oong ah-see-sanctum te)

Depicting Side Effects:

I'm feeling extremely unwell:
Estou me sentindo muito mal. (Ehs-toh meh sen-tee-ndo mwitoo mahl)

I have chest torment:
Estou com dor no peito. (Ehs-toh kohm dohr no peh-to)

I can't relax:
Não consigo respirar. (Presently kohn-see-goo reh-spee-rar)

Giving Individual Data:

I am [Your Name]:
Meu nome é [Seu Nome]. (May-oo noh-meh eh [Seu No-meh])

I'm a traveler:
Eu sou turista. (Eh-oo soh too-rees-tah)

Mentioning Quick Help:

If it's not too much trouble, help me rapidly:
Por favor, ajude-me rápido. (Por fah-vor, ah-joo-deh meh rah-pee-doo)

I really want clinical consideration now:
Preciso de atenção médica marketplace. (Preh-see-soh deh ah-ten-sawn meh-dee-kah ah-go-rah)

Giving Area Data:

I'm at [Your Location]:
Estou em [Sua Localização]. (Ehs-toh eng [Sua Loh-kah-lee-zah-sawn])

Communicating Torment or Distress:

It harms here:

Dói aqui. (Doy ah-kee)

I feel unsteady:
Estou tonto/a. (Ehs-toh tohn-toh/ah)

Looking for Help from Observers:

Might you at any point kindly call for help?:
Você pode chamar ajuda, por favor?
(Voh-say poh-de sha-damage ah-joo-dah,
por fah-vor)

Is there an emergency clinic close by?:
Tem um emergency clinic por perto? (Tem
oong os-pee-tahl poor pehr-to)

Portraying Sensitivities or Prescriptions:

I have sensitivity to [Specify Allergen]:
Eu tenho alergia a [Especificar alérgeno].
(Eh-oo ten-yoo ah-lehr-zhee ah
[Es-peh-see-charge kahr ah-lehr-zheh-no])

I take prescription for [Specify Condition]:
Eu tomo medicamento para [Especificar condição]. (Eh-oo toh-mo meh-dee-kah-men-toh pah-rah [Es-peh-see-expense kahr kohn-dee-sawn])

Cultural Tips:

Crisis Administration Number: In numerous Portuguese-talking nations, the crisis administration number is 112. Affirm the nearby crisis number and use it in the event of critical clinical circumstances.

Reporting Incidents to Authorities

On the off chance that you wind up expecting to report an occurrence to experts in a Portuguese-talking district, it's essential to impart obviously and smoothly. Here are expressions to help you in such circumstances:

Reaching Crisis Administrations:

I want to report an occurrence:
Preciso reportar um incidente. (Preh-see-soh reh-por-tar oong een-see-lair te)

Call the police, please:
Chame a polícia, por favor. (Sha-meh ah po-remains ee-ah, por fah-vor)

I've seen a mishap:

Testemunhei um acidente. (Tes-teh-moo-ney-ee oong ah-see-sanctum te)

Depicting the Occurrence:

There has been a burglary:
Houve um furto. (Gracious ve oong foohr-toh)

I saw somebody breaking into a vehicle:
Vi alguém arrombando um veículo. (Vee ahl-gwehng ah-rohm-bahn-doo oong veh-ee-koo-loh)

There is a fire:
Há um incêndio. (Ok oong een-sen-dee-oo)

Giving Area Data:

The occurrence happened at [Location]:

O incidente ocorreu em [Localização]. (O een-see-lair te goodness koh-reh-oo eng [Loh-kah-lee-zah-sawn])

I'm at [Your Location]:
Estou em [Sua Localização]. (Ehs-toh eng [Sua Loh-kah-lee-zah-sawn])

Mentioning Prompt Help:

Kindly come rapidly, it's a crisis:
Por favor, venha rápido, é uma emergência. (Por fah-vor, ven-ha rah-pee-doo, eh oo-mah ee-mehr-zhehn-syah)

I want assistance from the specialists:
Preciso de ajuda das autoridades. (Preh-see-soh deh ah-joo-dah dahs ah-toh-ree-dah-dees)

Giving Portrayals:

The suspect is [Description]:

O suspeito é [Descrição]. (Oos-spey-toh eh [Dehs-kree-sawn])

I didn't see the individual plainly, but...:
Não vi a pessoa claramente, mas... (Presently vee ah peh-soh-ah klah-rah-men-te, mahs...)

Communicating Concern:

I'm stressed over the wellbeing of others:
Estou preocupado/a com a segurança dos outros. (Ehs-toh preh-gracious koo-pah-doo/dah kohm ah seh-goo-rahn-sah dohs gracious tros)

Kindly send help straightaway:
Por favor, envie ajuda o mais rápido possível. (Por fah-vor, en-vee-eh ah-joo-dah oo mahys rah-pee-doo pos-see-vel)

Cultural Tips:

Keep even-headed: While detailing an occurrence, attempt to stay cool and give data as precisely as could be expected.

Language Boundary: If there's a language hindrance, attempt to utilize basic and clear sentences. Nearby specialists might have interpreters accessible.

Help out Specialists: Adhere to the directions of the specialists and give any extra data they might require.

Basic First Aid Terms

In the event of a crisis or while giving help, understanding fundamental medical aid terms in Portuguese can be essential.

General Terms:

Crisis:
Emergência (Eh-mehr-jen-syah)

Help!
Socorro! (So-koh-roh!)

Medical aid:
Primeiros socorros (Pree-mey-rohss soh-koh-rohss)

Normal Wounds:

Injury:
Lesão (Leh-sawn)

Dying:
Sangramento (Sang-grah-men-to)

Consume:
Queimadura (Kay-mah-doo-rah)

Crack:
Fratura (Frah-too-rah)

Sprain:
Torção (Tohr-sawn)

Gagging:
Engasgo (En-gahs-goo)

Seizure:
Convulsão (Kohn-vool-sow)

Activities and Guidelines:

Call a rescue vehicle:
Chame uma ambulância (Sha-meh oo-mah ahm-boo-lahn-syah)

Call the police:
Chame a polícia (Sha-meh ah po-remains ee-ah)

Rests:
Deite-se (Day-ee-teh-say)

Keep even headed:
Fique calmo/calma (Charge keh kahl-moo/kahl-mah)

Try not to move:
Não se mexa (Presently seh mey-shah)

Apply pressure:
Aplique pressão (Ah-plee-kay preh-ssawn)

Hoist the leg/arm:
Eleve a perna/braço (Eh-leh-veh ah pehr-nah/brah-so)

Inhale gradually:

Breathe devagar (Reh-spee-rey deh-vah-gahr)

Clinical Supplies:

Wrap:
Atadura (Ah-tah-doo-rah)

Bandage:
Look (Gah-zey)

Clean:
Antisséptico (Ahn-tees-sep-tee-koo)

Sticky tape:
Fita adesiva (Charge tah ah-deh-see-vah)

Scissors:
Tesoura (Teh-soh-rah)

Tweezers:
Pinça (Pee-za)

Requesting Help:

Is there a specialist close by?:
Tem um médico por perto? (Tem oong meh-dee-koo poor pehr-to)

Might you at any point help me?:
Você pode me ajudar? (Voh-say poh-deh meh ah-joo-dar)

I really want clinical help:
Preciso de assistência médica (Preh-see-soh deh ah-sees-ten-syah meh-dee-kah)

Portraying Side Effects:

I feel mixed up:
Estou tonto/tonta (Ehs-toh tohn-toh/tohn-tah)

I experience issues relaxing:

Tenho dificuldade para respirar (Ten-yoo dee-charge kool-dah-dee pah-rah rehs-peh-rahr)

My head harms:
Minha cabeça dói (Mee-nya kah-beh-sah doy)

Common Questions

Asking for Information

While looking for data in a Portuguese-talking climate, utilizing the right expressions can improve your correspondence.

General Requests:

Excuse me, could you at any point help me?:
Com licença, você pode me ajudar? (Kohm lee-sen-sah, voh-say poh-de meh ah-joo-dar)

I'm searching for data about...:
Estou procurando informações sobre... (Ehs-toh proh-koo-ran-do een-fohr-mah-sawn soo-bre)

Do you have at least some idea where I can find...?:
Você sabe onde posso encontrar...? (Voh-say sah-honey bee on-deh poh-so en-kon-trar)

Bearings:

Might you at any point let me know how to get to...?:
Você pode me dizer como chegar a...? (Voh-say poh-de meh dey-zer koh-moh sheh-gar ah)

Where is the nearest...?:
Onde fica o mais próximo...? (On-deh charge kah oo mahys proh-kssee-moh)

Is it nowhere near here?:
É longe daqui? (Eh grass geh dah-kee)

Opening times:

What time does [place] open/close?:
A que horas [local] abre/fecha? (Ok keh gracious ras [loh-kahl] ah-breh/feh-shah)

Is it safe to say that you are open at the end of the week?:
Vocês abrem nos balances de semana? (Vo-says ah-brehm nos feens dey weh-na)

Accessibility of Administrations:

Do you give [specific service]?:
Vocês oferecem [serviço específico]? (Vo-says gracious feh-reh-saym [ser-vee-soh es-peh-see-expense koh])

Is [service] accessible here?:
O [serviço] está disponível aqui? (Oo [ser-vee-soh] eh-stah dee-spo-nee-veyl ah-kee)

Costs and Installment:

What amount does it cost?:
Quanto custa? (Kwan-toh koos-tah)

Are there any limits?:

Tem algum desconto? (Tem ahl-goom dehs-kon-to)

Might I at any point pay with a Mastercard?: Posso pagar com cartão de crédito? (Poh-so pah-gar kohm kar-towm deh kreh-dee-to)

Explanation:

Might you at any point if it's not too much trouble, rehash that?:
Você poderia repetir, por favor? (Voh-say poh-dee-ree-ah reh-peh-teer, por fah-vor)

I didn't have the foggiest idea. Might you at any point make sense of it?:
Não entendi. Você pode explicar? (Presently ehn-high schooler dee. Voh-say poh-dey ehk-spee-kar)

Requesting Proposals:

What do you suggest?:

O que você recomenda? (Oo keh voh-say reh-koh-men-dah)

Is there a well-known spot to eat around here?:

Tem algum lugar famous para comer por aqui? (Tem ahl-goom loo-gahr po-crap lar pah-rah koh-mehr por ah-kee)

Time and Dates

Exploring time and dates in a Portuguese-talking climate is fundamental for powerful correspondence. Here are expressions to help you express and ask no time like the present related data:

Requesting the Time:

What time is it?:
Que horas são? (Keh goodness ras sah-o)

Do you have the opportunity?:
Você tem as horas? (Voh-say tehn ahs goodness ras)

Excuse me, might you at some point let me know the time?:
Com licença, você poderia me dizer as horas? (Kohm lee-sen-sah, voh-say poh-dee-ree-ah meh dey-zer ahs gracious ras)

Saying what time it is:

It's [specific time] o'clock:
São [hora específica] horas. (Sah-o [oh-ra es-peh-see-charge kah] goodness ras)

It's half past [hour]:
São meia hora. (Sah-o meh-ya gracious ra)

It's a quarter past/to [hour]:
São um quarto para [hora]. (Sah-o oong kwahr-toh pah-rah [oh-ra])

Days of the Week:

What day is it today?:
Que dia é hoje? (Keh dee-ah eh gracious je)

Today is [day]:
Hoje é [dia]. (Gracious je eh [dee-ah])

Tomorrow is [day]:

Amanhã é [dia]. (Ok mahn-yah eh [dee-ah])

Months and Dates:

What month is it?:
Que mês é este? (Keh mehs eh ehs-tey)

Today is the [day] of [month]:
Hoje é [dia] de [mês]. (Goodness je eh [dee-ah] dey [mehs])

What is the date today?:
Qual é an information de hoje? (Kwahl eh ah dah-tah dey gracious je)

Getting some information about Timetables:

When is [event/activity]?:
Quando é [evento/atividade]? (Kwan-doo eh [eh-ven-toh/ah-tee-vee-dah-deh])

What time does [place] open/close?:

A que horas [local] abre/fecha? (Ok keh gracious ras [loh-kahl] ah-breh/feh-shah)

Is [place] open on [day]?:
O [local] está aberto no [dia]? (Oo [loh-kahl] eh-stah ah-behr-toh noo [dee-ah])

Making Arrangements:

How about we meet on [day] at [time]:
Vamos nos encontrar na [dia] às [hora]. (Vah-mos nohs en-kohn-trar nah [dee-ah] ahss [oh-ra])

Might it be said that you are free on [day]?:
Você está disponível no [dia]? (Voh-say eh-stah dee-spo-nee-veyl noo [dee-ah])

Articulations of Time:

Morning:
Manhã (Mahn-yah)

Evening:
Tarde (Tahr-dey)

Evening/Night:
Noite (Noy-tey)

Weather Conversations

Understanding climate-related phrases is fundamental for ordinary discussions and travel arranging in Portuguese-talking districts.

Getting some information about the Climate:

How is the climate today?:
Como está o beat hoje? (Koh-moh eh-stah ooh tehm-crap gracious je)

What's the conjecture for later?:
Qual é a previsão para amanhã? (Kwahl eh ah preh-vee-zaw pah-rah ah-mahn-yah)

Is it will rain later?:
Vai chover mais tarde? (Vah-ee sho-vehr mah-ees lahr-dey)

Portraying Atmospheric conditions:

It's radiant:
Está ensolarado. (Ehs-tah
en-soh-lah-rah-doo)

It's overcast:
Está nublado. (Ehs-tah noo-blah-doo)

It's stormy:
Está chovendo. (Ehs-tah sho-vehn-doo)

It's blustery:
Está ventando. (Ehs-tah vehn-tahn-doo)

It's virus:
Está frio. (Ehs-tah free-yoo)

It's hot:
Está quente. (Ehs-tah kehn-tey)

Asking About Temperature:

What is the temperature today?:

Qual é a temperatura hoje? (Kwahl eh ah teh-mpeh-rah-too-rah goodness je)

Is it generally this hot/cold?:
É geralmente assim quente/frio? (Eh zheh-rahl-mehn-tee ah-appear kehn-tey/free-yoo)

What's the high/low temperature?:
Qual é a temperatura máxima/mínima? (Kwahl eh ah teh-mpeh-rah-too-rah mahk-see-mah/mee-nee-mah)

Getting ready for Climate:

Would it be advisable for me to bring an umbrella?:
Devotional trazer um guarda-chuva? (Deh-vo tra-yer oong gahr-dah-shoo-vah)

Do I really want a coat?:
Preciso de um casaco? (Preh-see-soh deh oong kah-sah-koo)

Will it be cold this evening?:
Vai fazer frio esta noite? (Vah-ee fah-zer free-yoo eh-stah noy-tey)

Communicating Inclinations:

I love radiant days:
Adoro dias ensolarados. (Ok doh-roh dee-as en-soh-lah-rah-dooz)

I favor cooler climate:
Prefiro um clima mais fresco. (Preh-expense roo oong kleeh-mah mahys freh-skoo)

I partake in the downpour:
Gosto da chuva. (Gohs-toh dah sho-va)

Traveling and Sightseeing

Expressions for Tourist Attractions

While investigating vacation destinations in Portuguese-talking areas, utilizing the right articulations can upgrade your experience.

Requesting Data:

What are the high priority attractions around here?:

Quais são as atrações imperdíveis nesta cidade? (Kwahy sah-o as ah-trah-sawngs eem-pehr-dee-veh-ees nehs-tah see-dah-dey)

Might you at any point suggest any verifiable destinations?:

Você pode recomendar algum lugar histórico? (Voh-say poh-dey reh-koh-mehn-dar ahl-goom loo-gahr ee-stoh-ree-koo)

Where is the closest vacationer data focus?:

Onde fica o centro de informações turísticas mais próximo? (On-deh expense kah oo sen-troo deh een-fohr-mah-sawns too-ris-tee-kas mahys proh-kssee-moh)

Appreciating Attractions:

This spot is wonderful!
Este lugar é lindo! (Ehs-tey loo-gahr eh leen-doo)

The engineering here is astonishing:
An arquitetura aqui é incrível. (Ok ar-kee-teh-too-rah ah-kee eh een-kree-vehl)

I'm dazzled by the normal magnificence:
Estou impressionado/a com a beleza normal. (Ehs-toh eem-preh-see-o-nah-doo/dah kohm ah beh-leh-zah nah-too-rahl)

Getting some information about Tickets and Entry:

How much is the extra charge?:
Quanto custa an entrada? (Kwan-toh
koos-tah ah en-trah-dah)

Is there a markdown for
understudies/seniors?:
Há desconto para estudantes/idosos? (Ok
dehs-kon-toh pah-rah
es-too-dan-tes/ee-doh-sos)

Are cameras permitted inside?:
Câmeras são permitidas lá dentro?
(Kah-meh-rahs sah-o pehr-mee-tee-dahs lah
dehn-troo)

Communicating Happiness:

I'm living it up by investigating:
Estou me divertindo muito explorando.
(Ehs-toh meh dee-ver-high schooler doo
mwitoo eks-ploh-ran-doo)

The view from here is amazing:
A vista daqui é de tirar o fôlego. (Ok vees-tah dah-kee eh dey tee-rahr oo foh-leh-goo)

I energetically suggest visiting this spot:
Eu recomendo muito visitar este lugar. (Eh-oo reh-koh-men-doo mwitoo vee-zee-tar eh-stey loo-gahr)

Getting Bearings:

How would I get to [attraction] from here?:
Como chego a [atração] a partir daqui? (Koh-moh sheh-goo ah [ah-trah-sawn] ah standard teenj dah-kee)

Is it inside strolling distance?:
É possível ir a pé? (Eh pos-see-vel eer ah pey)

What direction is the [attraction]?:

Por qual caminho fica [atração]? (Por kwahl kah-mee-nyoo charge kah [ah-trah-sawn])

Offering Thanks:

Much thanks to you for the proposal, it was phenomenal:
Obrigado/a pela recomendação, foi fantástico. (Goodness bree-gah-doo/dah peh-lah reh-koh-mehn-dah-sawn, foi fan-tahs-tee-koo)

I'm thankful for the potential chance to visit such a brilliant spot:
Sou grato/a pela oportunidade de visitar um lugar tão maravilhoso. (Soh grah-as well/dah peh-lah gracious por-too-nee-dah-dee dey vee-zee-tar oong loo-gahr tah-o mah-rah-vee-loh-so)

This experience is extraordinary:
Esta experiência é inesquecível. (Ehs-tah eks-peh-ree-ehn-syah eh een-ehs-keh-veel)

Talking About Activities

While examining exercises in a Portuguese-talking climate, utilizing the right articulations can assist you with taking part in discussions and making arrangements. Here are expressions to communicate and ask about different exercises:

Getting some information about Side interests:

What are your side interests?:
Quais são seus leisure activities? (Kwahy sah-o se-oos gracious honey bees)

Do you appreciate [specific activity]?:
Você gosta de [atividade específica]? (Voh-say gohs-tah deh [ah-tee-vee-dah-deh es-peh-see-expense kah])

I like to [activity] in my available energy:

Eu gosto de [atividade] no meu beat livre. (Eh-oo gohs-toh deh [ah-tee-vee-dah-deh] noo meh-oo tey-em-crap lee-vrey)

Arranging Exercises:

Might you want to [activity] this end of the week?:
Gostaria de [atividade] neste fim de semana?   (Gos-ta-ree-ah   deh [ah-tee-vee-dah-deh] nehs-teh feem dey weh-na)

We should go [activity] together:
Vamos fazer [atividade] juntos. (Vah-mos fah-zer [ah-tee-vee-dah-deh] joo-toos)

What do you want to do today?:
O que você tem vontade de fazer hoje? (Oo keh voh-say tehn vohn-tah-dee deh fah-zer goodness je)

Communicating Inclinations:

I love [activity]:
Eu amo [atividade]. (Eh-oo ah-moh [ah-tee-vee-dah-deh])

I hate [activity]:
Não sou fã de [atividade]. (Presently soh fahn deh [ah-tee-vee-dah-deh])

I favour [activity] in the first part of the day/evening:
Prefiro [atividade] de manhã/à noite. (Preh-expense roh [ah-tee-vee-dah-deh] deh mahn-yah/ah noy-tey)

Examining Sports:

Do you follow any games?:
Você acompanha algum esporte? (Voh-say ah-kom-pah-nyah ahl-goom es-por-tey)

I appreciate playing/watching [sport]:

Gosto de jogar/assistir [esporte]. (Gohs-toh deh zho-gar/ah-sees-teer [es-por-tey])

Who is your most loved [team/player]?:
Quem é seu time/jogador favorito? (Kwem eh se-o tey-me/zho-gah-dor fah-voh-ree-to)

Suggesting Relaxation Exercises:

You ought to attempt [activity], it's good times:
Você deveria experimentar [atividade], é divertido. (Voh-say deh-ve-ree-ah eks-pehr-ee-men-tar [ah-tee-vee-dah-deh], eh dee-ver-tee-doo)

Assuming that you like [activity], you'll adore [place/event]:
Se você gosta de [atividade], vai adorar [lugar/evento]. (Seh voh-say gohs-tah de [ah-tee-vee-dah-deh], vai ah-doh-rahr [loo-gar/eh-ven-to])

There's an incredible [activity] spot close to here:

Tem um ótimo lugar para [atividade] perto daqui. (Tem oong goodness tee-moo loo-gar pah-rah [ah-tee-vee-dah-deh] pehr-to dah-kee)

Describing Places

At the point when you need to share your impressions or ask about an area in a Portuguese-talking climate, it is vital to utilize graphic language.

Positive Portrayals:

This spot is shocking/wonderful:
Este lugar é deslumbrante/lindo. (Ehs-tey loo-gahr eh dez-loom-brahn-te/leen-doo)

The landscape here is stunning:
A paisagem aqui é de tirar o fôlego. (Ok pah-ee-sah-zhah ah-kee eh dey tee-rahr oo foh-leh-goo)

It's a beguiling/beautiful spot:
É um lugar encantador/adorável. (Eh oong loo-gahr en-kahn-ta-dor/ah-dor-ah-vel)

Negative Depictions:

This spot is packed/uproarious:
Este lugar está cheio/barulhento. (Ehs-tey loo-gahr eh-stah chey-oo/bah-roo-yen-to)

It's a piece grimy/chaotic:
Está um pouco sujo/desarrumado. (Ehs-tah oong poh-koo soo-zhoo/deh-sah-roo-mah-doo)

The roads are tight/turbulent:
As ruas são estreitas/caóticas. (Ahs roo-ahs sah-o es-three pointer tahs/kah-goodness tee-kahs)

Impartial Depictions:

It has a vivacious climate:
Tem uma atmosfera animada. (Tem oo-mah ah-toh-mehs-feh-rah ah-nee-mah-dah)

The engineering is fascinating:

An arquitetura é interessante. (Ok ar-kee-teh-too-rah eh een-teh-rehs-sahn-tey)

It's a tranquil/calm spot:
É um lugar tranquilo/silencioso. (Eh oong loo-gahr trahn-kwee-loo/see-lehn-syo-zoo)

Asking about Particulars:

What could be seen/done around here?:
O que há para ver/fazer por aqui? (Oo keh ah pah-rah veh/fah-zer poor ah-kee)

Are there any well known milestones close by?:
Há algum ponto turístico famoso por perto? (Ok ahl-goom pohyn-toh too-rees-tee-koo fah-moh-so poor per-toh)

Could you at any point suggest a decent café/bistro?:
Você pode recomendar um bom restaurante/bistro? (Voh-say poh-dey

reh-koh-mehn-dar   oong   boh
rehs-taw-rahn-teh/ka-fei)

Communicating Inclinations:

I lean toward places with a great deal of vegetation:
Prefiro lugares com muita vegetação. (Preh-charge roo loo-gahr-es koh-m moo-ee-tah veh-zhey-tah-sawn)

I like spots with dynamic nightlife:
Gosto de lugares com uma vida noturna vibrante. (Gohs-toh de loo-gahr-es kohm oo-mah vee-dah noo-teer-nah vee-brahn-tey)

I appreciate places with verifiable importance:
Eu gosto de lugares com significado histórico. (Eh-oo gohs-toh deh loo-gahr-es kohm see-nee-charge kah-doo his-toh-ree-koo)

Useful Phrases
for Technology

Communicating in a Digital World

In the present computerized age, successful correspondence stretches out to online connections. Whether you're exploring web-based entertainment, sending messages, or taking part in virtual discussions, these Portuguese expressions will assist you with imparting in the computerized world:

Online Entertainment Connections:

How would I follow you on [social media platform]?:
Como posso te seguir no [plataforma de mídia social]? (Koh-moh poh-so tey seh-gir noo [plah-tah-for-mah deh mee-dee-ah soh-see-ahl])

I loved your post/photograph:
Gostei da sua postagem/foto. (Gohs-tey dah soo-ah poh-stah-zhah/fotoo)

Did you see my message/remark?:
Você viu a minha mensagem/comentário?
(Voh-say vee-oo ah mai-nyah meh-sah-zhah/ko-men-tah-ree-oo)

Email Correspondence:

I'm writing to ask about [subject]:
Estou escrevendo para perguntar sobre [assunto]. (Ehs-toh es-krey-ven-doo pah-rah pehr-hooligan tar gracious breh [ah-soon-to])

Kindly track down connected the [document/file]:
Por favor, encontre em anexo o [documento/arquivo]. (Por fah-vor, en-kon-treh ehm ah-nehk-so o [doh-koo-men-toh/ar-kee-vo])

Much obliged to you for your brief reaction:

Obrigado/a pela sua resposta rápida. (Goodness bree-gah-doo/dah peh-lah soo-ah reh-spos-tah rah-pee-dah)

Virtual Gatherings and Calls:

Could we at any point plan a virtual gathering?:
Podemos agendar uma reunião virtual? (Poh-deh-mos ah-gehn-dar oo-mah rey-oo-nyown vee-rtu-ahl)

I will join the web-based gathering at [time]:
Eu vou participar da conferência online às [hora]. (Eh-oo promise pahr-tee-pee-ar dah kon-feh-ren-syah on-lahyn ahss [oh-ra])

Apologies, I was quiet. Could you at any point hear me now?:
Desculpe, eu estava no mudo. Você pode me ouvir public square? (Dehs-kool-peh, eh-oo es-tah-vah noo moo-do. Voh-say poh-de meh oo-go ah-go-rah)

Web-based Shopping:

I might want to submit a request for [product]:
Eu gostaria de fazer um pedido de [produto].
(Eh-oo gohs-tah-ree-ah deh fah-zer oong peh-jee-doo de [proh-doo-toh])

Is there a rebate code accessible?:
Tem algum código de desconto disponível?
(Tem ahl-goom koh-dee-goo deh dehs-kon-toh dee-spo-nee-veyl)

Technical support:

I'm disliking [device/software]:
Estou com problemas no [dispositivo/software]. (Ehs-toh kohm proh-bleh-mahs noo [dee-spee-zee-tee-voh/sof-twah-re])

Might you at any point if it's not too much trouble, help me with investigating?:
Você poderia me ajudar com a solução de problemas? (Voh-say poh-dee-ah meh ah-joo-dar kohm ah soh-loo-sawn deh proh-bleh-mahs)

Network protection Mindfulness:

Be careful of phishing messages and tricks:
Tenha cuidado com messages de phishing e golpes. (Ten-ha koo-ee-dah-doo kohm ee-mayls deh fih-shing ee gohl-peys)

Keep your passwords secure and remarkable:
Mantenha suas senhas seguras e únicas. (Mah-ten-ha soo-ahs se-nyahs seh-goo-ras ee oo-nee-kas)

Communicating Advanced Manners:

Many thanks to you for the convenient reaction:
Obrigado/a pela resposta oportuna. (Goodness bree-gah-doo/dah peh-lah reh-spos-tah gracious por-too-nah)

I value your brief thoughtfulness regarding this matter:
Agradeço pela sua atenção rápida an este assunto. (Ok grah-deh-soh peh-lah soo ah-ten-sawn rah-pee-dah ah eh-stey ah-soon-to)

Kindly let me know as to whether you want any additional data:
Por favor, me avise se precisar de mais informações. (Por fah-vor, meh ah-vee seh preh-see-dar dey mah-is een-fohr-mah-sawn)

Language
Survival Tips

Exploring another language, particularly while venturing out to a Portuguese-talking locale, can be both invigorating and testing. Here are some language endurance tips to help you convey actually and capitalize on your experience:

Learn Essential Expressions:
Begin with fundamental expressions like good tidings, thank you, if it's not too much trouble, excuse me, and essential conversational articulations. This establishment will go far in everyday associations.

Heft around this Phrasebook:
Keep this pocket-sized Portuguese phrasebook convenient. It very well may be a speedy reference guide for normal circumstances and crises.

Embrace Non-Verbal Correspondence:

Comprehend that non-verbal prompts like signals and looks are a general language. Focus on non-verbal communication to upgrade your comprehension.

Practice Elocution:
Centre around right elocution. Portuguese elocution can be testing, so rehearsing individual sounds and words is vital.

Inundate Yourself:
Submerge yourself in the language by watching Portuguese motion pictures, paying attention to music, and perusing basic texts. This openness assists you with getting familiar with the musicality and rhythm of the language.

Be Patient and Tenacious:
Language learning takes time. Show restraint toward yourself, celebrate little triumphs, and endure in your endeavours.

Each endeavour to convey is a step in the right direction.

Learn Key Cultural Standards:
Get to know fundamental cultural standards and customs. Pleasantness and cultural awareness will upgrade your collaborations and make you more invited.

Request Explanation:
Make it a point to for explanation on the off chance that you don't grasp something. The vast majority value the work and will help.

Ace Fundamental Travel Expressions:
Learn phrases connected with movement, like requesting bearings, requesting food, and looking for help in crises. These useful expressions are significant during your excursion.

Remain Positive and Liberal:

Move toward language learning with a positive mentality. Embrace the test and view every cooperation as an amazing chance to get to the next level.

Memory Aid Techniques

Learning another language includes remembering jargon, punctuation rules, and cultural subtleties. Here are memory help procedures to improve your language growth opportunity, particularly while learning Portuguese:

Memory helpers:
Make memory helpers to connect new words with recognizable ideas or sounds. For instance, partner the Portuguese word "sol" (sun) with the English word "sun powered."

Visual Affiliations:
Partner words with pictures. Make mental pictures that interface the significance of a word with its visual portrayal. This is especially viable for things and articles.

Lumping:
Separate long sentences or expressions into more modest lumps. Centre around learning

and recollecting that each lump in turn. This approach makes complex data more sensible.

Rhyming and Musicality:
Use rhyming words or make musical examples to recall data. This procedure is useful for recalling expressions and sentences with a melodic stream.

Cheat sheets:
Use cheat sheets to support jargon. Compose the Portuguese word on one side and the English interpretation on the other. Routinely survey the cheat sheets to reinforce memory.

Word Affiliations:
Partner new words with words you know in your local language. Make mental connections between the new and natural, making it simpler to review.

Narrating:

Make brief tales or situations that include the words you're attempting to recall. The story setting gives an important structure to learning.

Abbreviations and Acrostics:

Structure abbreviations or acrostics to recall arrangements of words or ideas. Make a sentence where the main letter of each word compares to the data you need to review.

Redundancy and Survey:

Redundancy is vital to memory. Routinely survey and practice what you've realized. This builds up brain associations and helps move data from the present moment to long-haul memory.

Mind Guides:

Make mind guides to address connections between words or ideas outwardly. This visual association supports reviewing data and grasping the design of the language.

Utilize the Memory Castle Strategy:
Partner words with explicit areas in a recognizable spot, similar to your home. As you intellectually travel through these areas, review the related words. This technique is particularly successful for retaining groupings.

Practice with Certifiable Settings:
Apply new words and expressions in genuine settings. Participate in discussions, compose short sentences, or mark objects in your current circumstance with their Portuguese names.

Record Yourself:
Record yourself communicating in Portuguese and pay attention to the accounts. Hearing your voice utilizing the

language supports articulation and helps memory.

Printed in Great Britain
by Amazon

42387712R00089